JACK SHIT

JACK SHIT

Summersdale Publishers Ltd
46 West Street
Chichester
West Sussex
PO19 1RP
UK

www.summersdale.com

Printed and bound in Czech Republic

ISBN: 978-1-84953-171-9

Substantial discounts on bulk quantities of Summersdale books are available to corporations, professional associations and other organisations. For details contact Summersdale Publishers by telephone: +44 (0) 1243 771107, fax: +44 (0) 1243 786300 or email: nicky@summersdale.com.

JACK SHIT

The Ultimate in Toilet Humour

TREVOR DE SILVA & STEVE ALLEN

summersdale

Jack shit

Holy shit

No shit

Shit hits the fan

Oh shit

Shit head

Shit-faced

Shit hot

Shit creek

Deep shit

Bad shit

Good shit

Serious shit

Stupid shit

Chicken shit

Eat shit

Prize shit

Weird hippy shit

Heavy shit

Little shit

Miserable little shit

Nasty little shit

Full of shit

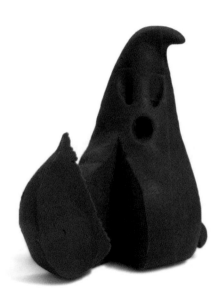

Piece of shit

In the shit

**Sooooo
in the shit**

Give a shit

Shit off a shovel

Feel like shit

Crock of shit

Sack of shit

Sea of shit

Drowning in a sea of shit

Shit heap

100%

crapola on crusty brown

Shit sandwich

Shit stirrer

Polishing a turd

Shit-scared

Right royally shat on

Shit storm

Get your shit together

Shat upon from on high

Now wash your hands

www.summersdale.com